YOU CAN BE
An Effective Sunday School Superintendent

How a general superintendent
can lead his Sunday School better,
by seeing and meeting
more of its needs

KENNETH O. GANGEL

Updated, expanded from *The Effective Sunday School Superintendent*

VICTOR BOOKS
a division of SP Publications, Inc.
WHEATON, ILLINOIS 60187

Offices also in Fullerton, California • Whitby, Ontario, Canada • Amersham-on-the-Hill, Bucks, England

Bible quotations are from the *King James Version* unless otherwise indicated. Another version quoted is the *New International Version* (NIV), © 1978 by New York Bible Society International. Used by permission.

ISBN: 0-88207-141-6

© 1981 by SP Publications, Inc. All rights reserved
Printed in the United States of America

VICTOR BOOKS
A Division of SP Publications, Inc.
P.O. Box 1825 • Wheaton, Illinois 60187

Offices also in Fullerton, California • Whitby, Ontario, Canada • Amersham-on-the-Hill, Bucks, England

Contents

Preface **7**
1 The Superintendent as Administrator **9**
2 The Superintendent as Recruiter **17**
3 The Superintendent as Personnel Manager **28**
4 The Superintendent as Communicator **37**
5 The Superintendent as Planner **45**
6 The Superintendent as Change Agent **53**
Conclusion **61**
Additional Resources **63**

To Sunday School superintendents
I have known
in evangelical churches
all across North America
and around the world

Preface

Churches come in all sizes, denominations, and geographical locations. Even within evangelical Christianity their emphases and distinctives vary greatly. But almost all of them have Sunday Schools. And almost all of those Sunday Schools have at their head a leader whom most call the "General Superintendent." To be sure, like their churches, these Sunday Schools differ in many ways, and the variety among the superintendents would be some sight indeed!

But when all the differences have been accumulated and accounted for, the task of the Sunday School superintendent as we enter these last years of the 20th century is amazingly singular. He may be leading a Sunday School of 10 students with 2 teachers or 10,000 students with a multitude of teachers—but the elements which make up the job show a great deal of similarity.

Several years ago we surveyed representative Sunday School superintendents. The reason for the survey was to see what superintendents are doing, what they think their needs are, and how we can help them make their job a bit easier and their leadership more effective. Based on the returns, I have prepared this book. Its purpose: to provide practical guidelines for the superintendent in carrying out his leadership role.

1
The Superintendent as Administrator

The superintendent is the administrator of the Sunday School. He may also be a teacher (though most are not). But even if he/she is a teacher, that is not his major responsibility. As superintendent he faces the tasks of leading, delegating, organizing, planning, initiating, evaluating, recruiting, and of course, supervising—all component parts of administration. As is commonly said, administration is getting things done through other people, and that is precisely the task of a superintendent. His "employees" are the members of his staff—teachers, secretaries, registrars and record keepers, assistant and departmental superintendents, and perhaps a Sunday School committee.

Of the superintendents surveyed, 94% agreed that their task was "administrative in nature and scope," 89% indicated they had training in administration either at the church or in business, and 71% felt that they have the spiritual gift of administration (see 1 Cor. 12:28, NIV).

Gift of Administration
Let's talk about the gift of administration first. As a matter of fact, only one superintendent responding to the survey indi-

cated he did not have the gift of administration. Several indicated they were not sure, but as already noted, well over two-thirds felt they were operating with that spiritual gift. This represents a great step forward in positive attitudes toward church ministry. About 10 years ago we would not likely have gotten anything near that kind of response. Many people would have thought of administration as unspiritual, for very little had been written or spoken about the gift of administration.

This is an important point for any effective Sunday School superintendent. It follows on the quality of his spiritual life and his continuing fellowship with the Lord. He must recognize that he faces the task of administration and ask himself (and the Lord) whether he has been equipped with the gift of administration. Ideally, this question should be answered before one allows himself to be elected or appointed to the task, but we do not always work with the ideals.

How can you tell if the Holy Spirit has given you this gift? The only sure way is by a spiritual communication between God's Spirit and yours that this is the case. But other indicators are whether Christian brothers and sisters seem to feel that you do (perhaps this is what led them to elect you to the job); whether you enjoy the administrative aspects of your task (such as those in the first paragraph of this chapter); and whether God has blessed and is continuing to prosper your work as a superintendent.

Remember that a spiritual gift is not a full-blown ability to perform. It is a capacity to be developed. That is why it is important for you to read widely in church administration books (never before in the history of the church have we had such a wealth of literature on the subject) and to involve yourself in seminars, workshops, and other learning experience so that your gift of administration may be matured and polished. Of course, experience is also of great help. If you are a new superintendent you should not expect to be carrying out your task with the expertise acquired by a 10-year veteran.

Human Relations

A second guideline which might be helpful to the administrative aspect of your Sunday School leadership is a recognition of the importance of human relations. To whom are you directly responsible in the lines of authority in your organization? Most superintendents are responsible to the Christian Education Board or Committee, more specifically to its chairman. But almost as many are responsible directly to the pastor. A few of those surveyed indicated lines of authority to other boards, such as elders or deacons, or to a full-time Director of Christian Education.

The person to whom you are responsible depends on the way your Sunday School is organized. Most church education experts agree that coordination of the total church education program is best carried out when a coordinating board or committee takes responsibility. The superintendent is on that committee, or at least directly responsible to it. In any case, learn to follow the lines of authority carefully. Know the person or group you answer to, and communicate on a regular basis.

There seems to be a new emphasis on group leadership in the church of the 1980s. This is in agreement with the New Testament, unlike the bureaucratic institutionalism which has greatly deterred corporate leadership throughout most of the history of the church. So commit yourself to being a team leader, not a demanding autocrat.

Span of Control

The lines of authority run two ways. It is just as important to know the people who are responsible to you as to know those over you, for you must exercise supervision of the former's work. This is called "span of control." A general guideline goes like this: *you're facing trouble if your span of control shows up in double figures.*

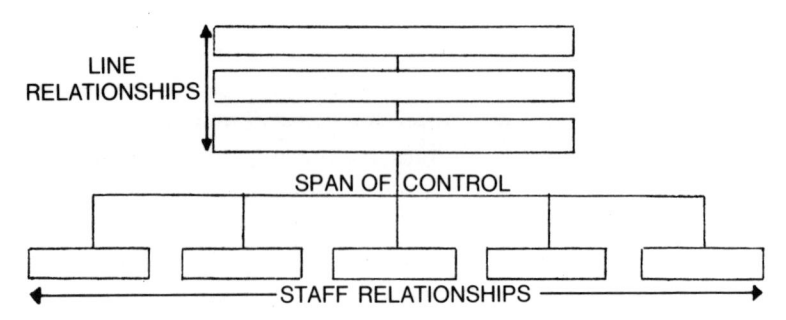

```
LINE
RELATIONSHIPS
            SPAN OF CONTROL
    ←——————— STAFF RELATIONSHIPS ———————→
```

Many superintendents are creating difficulties for themselves on this point. Unless your school is very small, you should have departmental superintendents who serve the role of "middle management" between you and the teaching staff. If you do not work with departmental superintendents, you may find yourself trying to supervise the work of 20 or 30 teachers directly. This dilutes both your control and your supervisory capabilities to a frightening degree.

Notice the chart, above. You could vary the number of teachers from three to nine depending on the size of the Sunday School, but the span of control of the superintendent would stay the same and the span of control for each departmental superintendent would be manageable as well. Of course, the same principle of administration relates to departmental superintendents. (They may never notice it unless you call it to their attention.)

Cooperative Ministry

Still another aspect in the total task of administration is your awareness of relationships with other leaders in the church and Sunday School. It would be an administrative and spiritual disaster for the Sunday School superintendent to be in conflict with the pastor, the director of Christian education (or the chairman of the board of Christian education or its members), any elder or deacon, or any member of his staff.

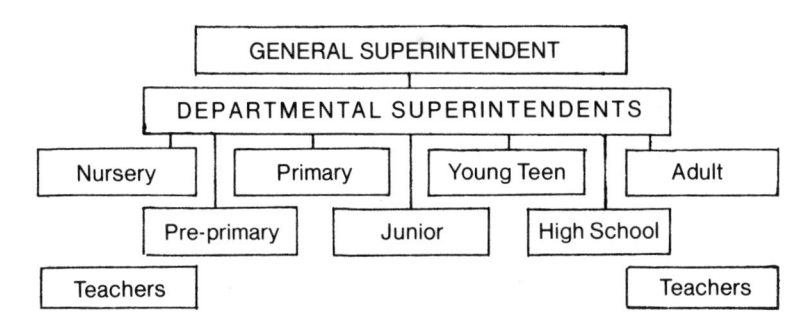

```
                    ┌─────────────────────────────┐
                    │   GENERAL SUPERINTENDENT    │
                    └──────────────┬──────────────┘
                    ┌──────────────┴──────────────┐
                    │ DEPARTMENTAL SUPERINTENDENTS│
                    └┬──────────┬──────────┬─────┬┘
          ┌─────────┐ ┌────────┐ ┌──────────┐ ┌───────┐
          │ Nursery │ │Primary │ │Young Teen│ │ Adult │
          └─────────┘ └────────┘ └──────────┘ └───────┘
              ┌───────────┐ ┌────────┐ ┌───────────┐
              │Pre-primary│ │ Junior │ │High School│
              └───────────┘ └────────┘ └───────────┘
          ┌──────────┐                        ┌──────────┐
          │ Teachers │                        │ Teachers │
          └──────────┘                        └──────────┘
```

The New Testament teaches a cooperative approach to ministry. As people serve the Lord they are also involved with serving one another (1 Cor. 12; 1 Thes. 2:7-12; Eph. 4:11-16).

Mutual submission is essential in the service of the Lord. Yes, you are the leader of the Sunday School, but the Apostle Paul indicates (Eph. 5:21) that you are to be in submission to your colleagues as well as they to you. Remember the emphasis of the Lord Jesus in the Upper Room just before His death: "I am among you as One who serves" (Luke 22:27, NIV). So the teamwork approach is the most important because it is biblical, but also because it offers the best approach to leadership and administration in the Sunday School.

Millions of dollars have been spent in management research in business and industry to discover what the Bible told us long ago, that a cooperative (sometimes called *democratic* or *participatory*) as opposed to one-man (sometimes called *autocratic*) philosophy of leadership is best. It provides a better maturing process for both the leader and the people who work with him. The superintendent and his staff grow spiritually by exercising spiritual gifts and by ministering mutually to each other as they serve the Lord together.

Proper Attitudes

The teamwork approach to administration can never be fully attained, however, until all people involved develop proper attitudes toward the crucial elements of ministry. This includes such things as:

(1) a biblical understanding of leadership as servanthood (Luke 22:24-27)

(2) a biblical understanding of how one should think of himself in relation to other believers (Phil. 2:1-5)

(3) a biblical practicing of the love ethic as described in 1 Corinthians 13

(4) a thorough understanding of the Lordship of Christ, which is one of the central themes of the entire New Testament.

These component parts of biblical administration are built through progressively learning a proper manner of operation. As your Sunday School's leader, you need to build mutual trust and respect within your staff and between them and other leaders of the congregation. Frequent and open interaction is vital.

Communicate regularly with your staff, both individually and as a group. Obviously, you will spend most of your time with those people who represent your "span of control," as Jesus spent most of His time with His 12 disciples. You are multiplying your ministry to the Sunday School through them.

Concentrate on the department superintendents and your immediate office staff (secretary, treasurer, registrar). Build your leadership ability into them, anticipating that one will be the next Sunday School superintendent. In spiritual security, without impatience or insecurity, advance their gifts and abilities as often and as far as you are able.

Remember the importance of accuracy in all your interpersonal communications. When Sir Walter Raleigh was in prison in the Tower of London, he decided to while away the hours by writing a history of the world. He had finished about 200 pages when he was interrupted by a great noise in the prison courtyard caused by a fight among some of the inmates. Raleigh and a number of others watched everything that happened. When the prisoners were assembled for mess at noon, you can imagine the major topic of conversation. Eight prisoners gave Raleigh their individual versions of the fracas and no two stories were the same. As soon as he was back in his cell after lunch, Raleigh took his manuscript of the history of the world, tore it into pieces, and threw it into the fire.

Let your communication be reliable.

Team Decision-Making

Finally, proper attitudes toward ministry are developed by a willingness of the leader (that's you) to rely on team decision-making (consensus judgment). In some ways a Christian organization such as a Sunday School is much like a small business or even a public elementary school in your town. But in other ways, it is completely different. The church is an *organization* but it is primarily as *organism*—the body of Christ. Consequently, if the Holy Spirit indwells every one of your people, He can help you be a better leader and decision-maker by the consensus wisdom you gain from them. On two occasions one of the wisest leaders who ever lived wrote, "In the multitude of counselors there is safety" (Prov. 11:14; 24:6).

The chapters which follow concentrate in greater detail on five aspects of the administrative task. But before we are ready to think in that specific detail, the general foundations of a distinctively Christian approach to administration are important. Of course, we have only begun to discuss this idea, and you would do well to read on this subject more widely. In fact, you should begin to build your own personal library of books on church administration. The bibliography on page 63 lists some of the best books and was prepared to be selective rather than exhaustive. Use it carefully.

Questions for Discussion

1. Describe the gift of administration and how it applies to a Sunday School superintendent.

2. Discuss the "lines of authority" in your Sunday School. Where and how do you fit in?

3. What is "span of control"? Name all persons presently in your span of control.

4. How does team decision-making fit into your administrative functions as they are presently carried out?

2
The Superintendent as Recruiter

One of the major hurdles most Sunday School superintendents face is the matter of personnel recruitment. In our recent survey, we asked about the problems or questions on which superintendents would most appreciate help. Of those responding, 37% said they would like suggestions in the general duties of administration, and 24% specifically indicated the issue of "personnel recruitment." These were write-in responses, not the selection of ideas already listed. Why is it that so many good Sunday Schools are often short of qualified workers?

Whose Job Is It?

The first question we have to answer has to do with the responsibility for recruitment. Even though some careful organizational setup, such as the Christian education board, may seek to involve a group of people in the recruiting task, the primary burden of responsibility falls on the superintendent himself.

But let's make a distinction between *deciding* on a worker and *asking* that worker. It seems that the first step, deciding, properly belongs in a group setting. Unilateral and arbitrary choices of people for tasks as important as Sunday School teaching should not be the responsibility of one person, no matter how good an administrator he or she might be. We need to be reminded of the selection of Matthias (Acts 1), of the seven "deacons" (Acts 6), and the appointment of the first missionaries (Acts 13). All three of these were *group actions*.

Work with the board of Christian education or Sunday School council in making appointments. If your church does not have such a group, do some study and present a recommendation to the appropriate authorities to get one started. A properly functioning board of Christian education will gather information on potential workers, know the total program of church ministry so that correlation can be effective in worker recruitment, list the opinions and counsel of various dedicated and spiritual leaders, and pray together for the will of God in their selections.

Making Contact

The actual contact needs to be made next. Usually a board of Christian education will designate the person responsible for the particular work in question to extend the invitation to a new worker. If a Sunday School is very large, the general superintendent might delegate that task to the departmental superintendent who is responsible for the area in which a vacancy or new post is being filled.

Generally speaking, we make three major errors in recruiting teachers and staff in the Sunday School:

1. We *recruit* too carelessly, without having carried out a thorough program of education which helps everyone in our church to understand that he has a responsibility before God to serve Christ through the church in some way.

2. We *ask* too carelessly, without sufficient time of investigation, prayer, and a concern for people's interests and spiritual gifts.

3. We *install* too carelessly, without clear-cut job descriptions, a definite tenure of appointment, or a regular evaluation of the new workers' achievements.

Seven Steps to Success

A number of churches have restructured their recruiting patterns and have become more productive in this area by following the seven steps suggested in the chapter on "Recruiting Workers in the Church," from my book *Leadership for*

Church Education. These seven steps are reproduced here with a brief paragraph of explanation for each. If you want further details, the book is listed on page 63.

1. Conduct a complete need and task survey. What the Christian education board needs to know about the entire educational program in the church, you need to know about the Sunday School. You need to have a written list of *every* position of ministry in the entire Sunday School, what qualifications that position calls for in a worker, and how soon it will need to be filled. Obviously, the initial thrust of such a survey is the hardest work, but keeping it up to date on a regular basis is also important.

2. Conduct a talent and ability survey. We might more properly call this a "gift and call survey." We want to know how people understand their spiritual gifts, what they believe God has called them to do in the church, and what experience they have in various types of ministry. Again, this is a continuing job since people are coming and going quite regularly in most churches. If your file of potential workers is up to date, you should have a very helpful resource to consult when specific recruitment faces you.

3. Continually promote and instruct people in the church's total educational task. Use the church bulletin, tackboards, monthly or quarterly mailings, posters, verbal announcements, and any other means at your disposal to let the entire congregation know what your Sunday School is doing. Get people excited about Sunday School. Enlist the help of your pastor in really generating enthusiasm for this important part of his church's educational ministry.

4. Relate every position to the ultimate goal of the church's educational program. Here you have to grapple with the matter of objectives. Is it a purpose of your Sunday School to win people to Christ? Is it a purpose of your Sunday School to build up Christians toward maturity? A biblical understanding of the Sunday School has to hold these two in almost equal balance. A school which is focusing too much on one or the other will lose its balance and tend to distort its program. In addition to these two central aims of *evangelism* and *edification,* your Sunday School also provides worship, fellowship, and opportunities for service. When we ask people to serve in the Sunday School, we need to show them this broad ministry and its value to the church.

5. *Make the approach person-centered.* Here is the important motto: *Ask specific people for specific jobs for specific lengths of time.* It is here that many of the superintendents surveyed are in trouble. Of the respondents to a question on the tenure of appointment for teachers, 51% indicated that appointments were for one year (that's good); but 36% indicated that appointments were "indefinite" (that's bad).

Person-centeredness is extremely important so that our people do not get the idea that they work *for* the superintendent. The story is told of two gardeners working for wealthy estates on Long Island who met one day at the local hardware store.

"I hear you're working for that banker fellow now," said one.

"Me, working for him? You've got it all wrong," replied the other. "He gets up at 5:30 every morning to get aboard an overcrowded, rickety train to commute to the hot city so he can keep up his estate and pay us our weekly wages. No, I'm not working for him; he's working for me."

And in the real sense that administration always serves the teaching process, you might say that the superintendent is really working for his teachers.

6. *Offer each potential worker a carefully prepared job analysis.* The job description must be specific enough for the potential worker to know what will be expected of him. Furthermore, the worker needs to know what he can expect from the superintendent as well. Then everyone knows where

he stands in the ministry of the Sunday School.
  7. Do not hurry the worker's decision. If we truly want God's will to be done, then we can leave in His hands the prospective worker's decision whether to accept the assignment. Let him study the job description and prayerfully consider his part in it. God's work must be done in God's timing.
  As Sunday School pro Harold J. Westing says, ". . . when teachers have a place of respect among the congregation . . . it becomes far easier to recruit the caliber of staff you desire. Churches which have maintained a proper standard for a period of time often find that they actually have a waiting list of people who would like to become teachers" (*The Super Superintendent,* Denver: Accent, 1980, p. 50).

How Long?
We can take a cue from other kinds of professional education on the length of worker appointments. Almost all teacher appointments from kindergarten through the highest level of graduate schools are made annually. True, most schools work with some form of permanency called "tenure," but that is only given to real professionals who have established themselves both by training and experience, and even that traditional system of tenure is now being increasingly challenged on many campuses as obsolete and inadequate.
  In the face of this evidence, why would any Sunday School ask a teacher to take a class on an indefinite basis? It just doesn't make sense. Are we really that sure of our appointments? Can we guarantee that the students will like the teacher and the teacher will do well with that age-level? What about the worker's awesome responsibility of being asked to say yes to a class that might occupy his time for the next 30 years?
  Appointments should be made annually. Of course, that doesn't mean that we completely change our staff every year,

any more than the local junior college completely changes its faculty. When teachers have performed well, they receive appointment for the next year, and then another, and another, so that the appointment extends through several years—but not automatically.

Help Stamp Out Quitters!

Another good feature of the annual appointment (if we handle it correctly) is the opportunity to impress on the teacher that an agreement to teach extends for at least one year. In other words, we don't want any dropouts three or four months after the curriculum year has begun.

Some churches find it helpful to conduct a significant public dedication service. Some also distribute written appointment notices or Certificate of Ministry sheets signed by the superintendent, the chairman of the Christian education board, and probably also the pastor. We do well to remind our workers of the words of the Lord Jesus to His Father concerning finishing one's job: "I have brought You glory on earth by completing the work You gave Me to do" (John 17:4, NIV). We must emphasize commitment when we do our recruiting:

PROSPECTIVE TEACHER: Yes, Tom, I really will consider your request regarding teaching that Junior High class. I can't tell you at this time whether I believe God wants me to do this, but I will pray about it and have an answer for you within two weeks.

SUPERINTENDENT: Thanks, Jack. We will be praying with you. The Board of Christian Education really felt that God led us to ask you and I am representing them in explaining the ministry of that class. By the way, we want you to know that all of our appointments are for at least one year. If you decide that God wants you to join with us in this important ministry of the Sunday School, we expect you to commit yourself to the class from the first Sunday in September of this year through the last Sunday in August of next year. At that time, all positions will

24 / You Can Be an Effective Sunday School Superintendent

Certificate of Ministry
Calvary Church of Hialeah

According to the call of God, by His Grace
and with the approval of the Christian Education Committee,

_____

has been appointed to serve as

_____

for one year from September 1, 19 _____ to August 31, 19 _____ .
May this period of ministry be marked by spiritual power, biblical dependability, and an attitude of cooperation with brothers and sisters in Christ.

God bless you!

_____
Pastor

_____ _____
Chmn., Christian Education Committee   Ministry Supervisor

be reviewed and appointments will be made for the following year.

How to Deal with Decliners

Of course, there will be times when people whom you ask to take on certain ministries in the Sunday School will politely decline. I have a standard response in such situations, especially if the person is not active in any ministry in the church. It sounds something like this: "Well, Bob, we certainly don't want you involved in any ministry which has not been affirmed by the Lord as His will. But I know you believe every Christian should be active in his local church somehow, so why don't you tell us what you'd like to do for the Lord in our congregation. I'll give you a couple more weeks on that one and check with you again. By the way, here's a book on spiritual gifts which might be helpful in ascertaining how God can use you along with the rest of us here in our church."

Training

Training is another important part of the task of recruiting. In one sense we don't train until after we have recruited. But in at least two important ways training is a part of recruiting. First, when we approach a potential worker we might have better success (as well as a better worker eventually) if we promise him some good training for the task we are asking him to undertake. Second, if we develop several good leadership training opportunities, such as classes or seminars, we can then recruit potential teachers from people who have already been through the training.

This is one reason we should generally not refer to such classes or seminars as "teacher training," but rather as "leadership training." When we use the first phrase people have a tendency to say, "That's not for me, I'm not a teacher." Then we have to convince them that someday they might be. But we can more easily communicate the idea that all adult Christians are leaders in one way or another (parents, for example, at home), and therefore the leadership training class is for everyone. From that class we hope to obtain Sunday School teachers as well as workers for other tasks in the church's educational program.

There is something to be said for knowledge, and we need to encourage people to take advantage of training opportunities. A small factory had to stop operations when an essential piece of machinery broke down. When no one could get it operating again, an outside expert was called. After looking over the situation for a minute, he took a hammer and gently tapped the machine in a certain spot. It immediately started running again.

When he submitted his bill for $100, the plant supervisor went into a rage and demanded an itemized statement. What he got read as follows: "For hitting the machine, $1; for knowing where to hit, $99."

Writing in a Superintendent's Christian Education Monograph published in Scripture Press Ministries, Dr. Roy B. Zuck suggests that "we must assure a new worker of our support, prayer, and appreciation." That can be done by various means:

1. A pastoral announcement
2. A dedication service, as mentioned earlier
3. A listing of new workers in the bulletin or in your church paper
4. An invitation to the annual appreciation banquet
5. Constant demonstration of appreciation by the superintendent

Recruitment can also be handled as a specialty ministry. One Midwestern church advances its leading educational officers on a three-year cycle—Sunday School superintendent to chairman of the Christian education board to personnel recruiter. And what a help the personnel recruiter is to the new superintendent!

Questions for Discussion

1. If your church has a Christian education committee, describe your relations with that group.

2. Review the "seven steps to success" in recruiting workers. How does your present process differ? What changes would be helpful?

3. Define five specific steps you will take this year to cut down on teacher dropouts.

4. Review your leadership training program. How can it be improved?

3
The Superintendent as Personnel Manager

Bill Warner hadn't been superintendent of First Church long before he discovered that recruiting teachers was only a small part of his total job. The recruiting process for a certain teacher might take days or even weeks, but the development and supervision of that teacher (referred to in administrative science as "personnel management") might be a process of many years.

People Problems
One of the basic issues at stake here is the recognition of what is involved in the supervisory process. Anyone who has responsibilities for the work of others will immediately discover that he is faced with some "people problems." The Sunday School superintendents in the survey listed some of these problems:
 1. Lack of faithfulness and commitment
 2. Failure to follow guidelines
 3. Unwillingness to accept responsibility
 4. Poor discipline of students
 5. Tardiness
 6. Breakdown of communication
 7. Difficulties in motivation

The results of field interviews on this point invariably indicate that too few leaders look for these problems *in themselves*. Leaders often tend to be self-referential only in a positive sense. They are just opposite of the hypochondriac lady who read medical magazines each month to see what exotic symptoms she might have. One day, however, she ran into an old country doctor who wouldn't put up with her nonsense.

"You couldn't possibly have the disease you say is destroying you," he observed. "In the first place, if you did have it, you'd never know it. It causes absolutely no pain or suffering whatever."

To which the lady responded, "There, you see! Those are my symptoms precisely."

Leaders should not imagine that every malfunction of the Sunday School staff is their personal failure. But they ought not to assume the opposite belief either—that they cannot be the ones at fault.

Components of Supervision

Supervision is a broad process, including in it a number of distinct elements.

1. A good supervisor knows how to delegate responsibility. In the case of a general superintendent, this delegation would be to staff assistants, departmental superintendents, committee members, secretaries or clerks, and in the case of a very small Sunday School, directly to teachers.

The classic biblical passage on the process of delegation is found in Exodus 18. You should study it carefully. Notice that delegation did not come naturally to Moses, that he delegated only to qualified leaders, and that everyone (including the leader) benefited from the change.

2. The supervisor must take responsibility for those who work under him and to whom he has delegated certain tasks. One of the biggest problems superintendents face is their constant dealing with people who don't want to take responsibility. Of course, that problem may or may not be a reflection of the superintendent's own tendency to "pass the buck" whenever possible. Leadership depends on a willingness to be a responsible person who will be accountable for the task assigned to him.

3. The supervisor must occasionally exercise discipline over his staff. The word *punishment* may not fit, though on some

occasions even that might be necessary. The term *discipline* identifies a more careful structure such as parents create in a family so that children can grow up under clearly defined guidelines of behavior. Obviously, the more mature the child the less rigid the discipline, until the child grows into a properly functioning adult who responds in self-discipline rather than being corralled by external forces.

But as personnel managers we cannot assume that people will always take care of their responsibilities themselves. It becomes necessary then to issue memos or carry out counseling sessions to gently encourage our people to get the job done. Emphasize *gently*.

Shortly after World War II a refugee from a displaced persons camp got his visa, sailed for America, and promised to send for his wife as soon as he had the money. Several months had gone by when he received a letter from her written in English. Unable to read English as yet, he asked a neighbor to read it to him. This man was a rather ill-tempered, gruff individual with a harsh voice who read, "Why haven't you sent for me? I need the money right away." The immigrant snatched the letter away and angrily put it in his pocket. How dare she speak to him that way when he was doing the best he could to earn the money?

A few weeks later he received a second letter. This time a young pastor read the letter to him. In a soft and patient voice he read, "Didn't you get my letter? Why haven't you sent for me? I need the money right away."

"Well, that's much better," responded the immigrant. "If she hadn't changed her tone, I would never have sent for her!"

Let's remember that when we face the administrative responsibility of discipline, our tone of voice and manner should make that moment redemptive rather than destructive.

4. The supervisor sets work standards, not necessarily on his own, but in cooperation with his staff. Bill Warner learned that

at First Church ideas and standards solicited from the teachers and workers were much better adhered to than those he had tried to "hand down" in the early days of his superintendency

It may be important to note that the word "standards" is used in a special sense when applied to Sunday School work. In the book mentioned earlier, Harold Westing suggests that "a Sunday School standard is an ideal measure by which is defined the quality of work and devotion expected of the Sunday School staff of workers. It serves as a guideline for procedures and priorities as well as an effective discipline tool, all of which most Christian education staff people need" (p. 144).

5. The supervisor is a team builder. Let's get back for a moment to what we were discussing in the last chapter about the cooperative ministry of the church. If we are to develop the kind of teamwork essential to the joyful carrying out of the ministry, all workers must know their tasks and believe that each task is important.

This sense of importance is conveyed by the leader. Not only must he establish clearly the importance of those within his span of control, but he must teach them how to communicate the sense of importance all the way down the line. That teacher in the preschool class next to the furnace room must have a feeling of significance in the group process—of being an integral part of the total Sunday School. To speak in theological terms, she must feel that 1 Corinthians 12, with its focus on the importance of all the parts of the body, is really working as far as she is concerned.

6. A supervisor must dish out both criticism and praise. The way you as a leader use commendation and condemnation can have a significant effect on the motivation of your workers. Quite obviously, constructive criticism is as important to a member of your staff as it is to you. It also ought to be obvious,

however, that he finds it just as difficult to receive criticism as you do. As a matter of fact, assuming your greater maturity and wider experience in being a follower as well as a leader, he probably finds it *more* difficult. So you must constantly work to maintain a spirit of unity and community among the staff by praising as often as possible and criticizing in a most constructive way, usually with a word of appreciation for some positive element of a member's performance included (Phil. 2:1-5).

Above all things, the work situation must be free from an atmosphere of intimidation and you must be careful never to manipulate workers, even when such manipulation might be the fastest way to achieve worthy ends. The evangelical community simply must insist that the end still does not justify the means, even though the social sciences give us some attractive means for getting people to do what we want:

7. The supervisor must handle grievances satisfactorily. "Teachers and workers tend to just give up when they become disenchanted with an institution or their work in it. A supervisor's response to a worker's grievances may very well retain the employee or alienate him completely. He must understand precisely what the worker's complaint is, if there is a satisfactory basis for the complaint, and if there is any precedent in the organization for handling this kind of complaint. It is important to assure the worker that prompt attention will be given to the issue and that corrections will be made if the organization is wrong" ("Personnel Selection and Supervision," *Competent to Lead,* Kenneth O. Gangel, Moody Press, Chicago, Ill.).

It is important for us to recognize that a statement of grievance is not a personal attack against the superintendent or even an attack against the organization. It may be an honest disagreement with policy or a reaction to a flagrant abuse of the worker by the Sunday School or one of its leaders.

Too often Christian leaders will not hear a grievance fairly but immediately identify that grievance as an expression of sin, emotional instability, or misunderstanding on the part of the worker. It may indeed be one of those three, but we need to examine every complaint to see whether the organization is in some way taking undue advantage of the worker, or whether something else needs to be corrected.

8. The supervisor must take responsibility for getting results. Goal achievement in the school ultimately rests with you. A goal may be numerical (too often we think only in these terms), or it may be the more important but harder-to-measure component of spiritual growth. But since administration is "getting things done through people," then "getting results" means facilitating the work of your staff so they can achieve what you have together agreed on as the goals of the Sunday School for a given period of time, such as a quarter or perhaps a year.

Motivation

The Sunday School superintendent is constantly faced with the necessity of motivating volunteer workers to carry out their tasks. This requires striking a responsive chord in many individuals. Motivation is not manipulation. It is rather the offering of good reasons for doing what you say needs to be done, or perhaps doing it in the way you suggest it ought to be done. You should do further reading in the area of motivation (see *Additional Resources,* p. 63) because you will be constantly faced with this component of the leadership role. The superintendent who has no understanding of the belongingness and love-needs, the esteem and recognition needs of church workers, will constantly be swimming upstream in his efforts to bring about positive motivation among his staff.

Surely we can also say that the more clearly you understand the goals of your Sunday School, the more readily and understandably you can communicate those goals to your staff. And probably the more thoroughly they will work with you in achieving those goals.

Motivation in church leadership must never be allowed to degenerate to the point of political favors or back-room bargaining. Our staff members are not working *for* us, nor are they ultimately responsible *to* us. In the lines of authority both we and they are ultimately responsible to Jesus Christ, the Head of the church. If we can somehow direct the orientation of our people to service for Him, we have taken a long and positive step along the road to motivation.

Disciple and Discipler

In his role of personnel manager, the superintendent is both a disciple and discipler. An emphasis on self-denial, cross-carrying, and faithful following are crucial in discipleship. A true disciple puts Christ before himself; he is willing to suffer difficulties because of his faith, and those around him can see what it means to follow Christ because of his example. This is not some unique plateau of spiritual experience but rather the posture that Christ wants from all of us, particularly those who have accepted the responsibilities of leadership. Humility is a built-in element of discipleship, and the Sunday School superintendent needs to pray fervently that humility will be demonstrated in his life and leadership (James 4:6).

The disciple then becomes a discipler. The example of Jesus is most refreshing as we watch Him work with His small band of 12 men. A careful reading of the four Gospels demonstrates that Jesus cared for His disciples first (John 11:11-15). The crowds were there, and He ministered to them effectively on a regular basis. But His primary concern was for His "staff."

Like the Lord Jesus, the Christian leader is always teaching, whether dealing with students or staff. The biblical discipler is always on the lookout for ways to build up and help his disciples. That is the way Jesus did it, and that is what He expects of us as leaders responsible for personnel management.

Cleveland Amory tells a story about Judge John Lowell of Boston. One morning the judge sat at breakfast, his face hidden in the morning paper as usual. A frightened maid tiptoes into the room and whispered something into Mrs. Lowell's ear. The message was obviously distressing to the lady and, after pausing for a moment to bolster her courage, she said, "John, the cook has burned the oatmeal and there is no more in the house. I am afraid that this morning, for the first time in 17 years, you will have to go without your oatmeal."

The judge responded without putting his paper down, "It's all right, my dear. Frankly, I never cared much for it anyhow."

What are we intentionally teaching those who observe our lives? If we don't care for oatmeal, perhaps we ought to say so.

Questions for Discussion

1. Define supervision. How are you presently exercising this important function of administration?

2. Four Scripture passages are mentioned in this chapter. Study each and analyze more thoroughly their impact on your leadership style.

3. What procedures does your Sunday School presently employ for handling grievances? How can they be improved?

4. How are you serving your staff as a discipler? What guidelines does the example of Jesus provide for you?

4
The Superintendent as Communicator

The superintendents in the survey were asked to rate their skills in communication on a scale of 1 to 10. Most seemed to be quite generous with themselves, indicating an average of 6.8 with 8 being the most frequently reported score. It is to be hoped that these scores are a true reflection of the general ability of Sunday School superintendents to communicate with their staffs, because communication is vital to success.

Communication is a strategic part of the total administrative process. Quite obviously the effectiveness of recruiting and supervising depends on your ability to get your ideas across. But communication is a two-way street. The effective administrator (superintendent) dare not be trapped into a pattern of monologue. He needs to understand what is happening in the classes and on the field so that future executive decisions can be related to the practical realities of the task and not to hazy unrealities perceived in his office.

Remember Bill Warner, from chapter 3? As Bill caught on to the task of recruitment and supervision, he quickly learned that communication is an essential part of his role on a day-to-day basis. In the process he learned that there were at least four major phases of interpersonal communication of which he had to be constantly aware: (1) words, (2) nonverbal communication (a smile, a frown, a nod of the head), (3) written communication, which we'll talk more about in this chapter, and (4) the art of listening to other people.

So let's approach the task of communication by using the "4-M Approach," meetings, memos, minutes, and moments. Too often we think about communication as some general process that cannot be pinned down. It is true that we must be aware of its process at all times, but the superintendent's administrative task requires him to communicate especially clearly at certain points in his ministry.

By the way, though communication is carried on the backs of vehicles we call *words,* the process itself depends on the sharing of *meanings.* You cannot judge the effectiveness of your communication by how many words you speak or even by how clear those words are. The important point is whether or not people understand what you mean.

The founder and generally recognized "high priest" of the general semantics movement is Alfred Korzybski. In his book, *Science and Sanity,* he uses a marvelous illustration in which he compares words to maps and the reality which words represent to the actual territory which the map depicts. He then follows with a pungent quote regarding verbal communication: *The map is not the territory.* What Korzybski means, of course, is that the use of a word is like the use of a map, not to be confused with the reality which the word represents. It's the *meaning* which the hearer places on the word that makes the difference.

Meetings

How often should a Sunday School staff meet? When asked that question on the survey, 60% of the superintendents said "monthly" (that's good). The second largest block (30%) said bimonthly. Whether these staffs actually meet that often may be questioned, but the responses do point up the thinking of the superintendents on the *need* for regular staff meetings.

How often should *you* meet with your staff? Perhaps after the school is functioning precisely the way it should be and you have settled into your administrative task with a year or two of experience behind you, bimonthly meetings would be satisfactory. But touching base with all your people at least once a month, for a period of time no matter how brief, is an important element in the communication process. A few Sunday School staffs may meet weekly, but that might introduce the burdensome task of multiple meetings.

When should your Sunday School staff meet? The answer to that question, of course, depends on the kind of schedule and calendar by which your church operates. One church finds it quite effective to hold its Sunday School meetings on the same evening as the monthly workers' conference. The first hour is given to general help for all different educational ministries, and during the second hour each church agency holds its own meetings, with the superintendent presiding over the Sunday School staff meeting at that time.

What should be done at a monthly staff meeting? Obviously, some business must be transacted, but there also ought to be a high level of inspiration and education. Ralph Heim encourages us to "view every formal monthly or quarterly meeting of teachers and officers as an educational opportunity." He offers several "practical principles to guide a leader in making the most of any group meeting":

Provide for something worthwhile to happen.
Be prepared with a program thought through and worked out.
Arrive early and start the meeting on time.
Win the members to the program; don't try to drive them.
Suit the occasion with appropriate dignity, reverence, or good
 humor.

Keep the program moving.
Don't talk too much; also listen.
Be tactful in handling difficult problems and persons.
Observe the special requirements of the particular type of meeting.
Achieve the chosen purpose as far as possible.
(*Leading a Church School,* Fortress Press, Philadelphia, Pa.)

In the survey, the superintendents indicated they spent their staff meeting time as follows, the figures in parentheses showing how the percentages would apply to a one-hour meeting:
Instruction 35% (21 minutes)
Planning 29% (17 minutes)
Business 20% (12 minutes)
Inspiration 16% (10 minutes)

How do you secure attendance at a Sunday School staff meeting? It may sound trite to say it, but people will come to something that can be shown to be genuinely helpful in a work to which they are committed. There are several levels or steps leading up to an attendance commitment of that kind. First, people must be committed to the task of Sunday School ministry under the call of God. Second, the staff meetings must be genuinely attractive and effective, terms which have technical definition in leadership studies.

"'Group effectiveness' is a term describing the extent to which groups reward their members. 'Group attractiveness,' on the other hand, refers to the extent to which they are *expected* to reward their members. Contemporary research tells us that the 'effects' in a group are accomplished in direct relationship to interaction or noninteraction" (Kenneth O. Gangel, *Leadership for Church Education,* p. 154).

In other words, people must *know* that they will be helped.
To achieve all this, a certain amount of quality publicity is

important. What the publicity should do is create a desire for the information to be presented at the staff meeting. When Ramsay MacDonald was Prime Minister of England, he was discussing with another government official the possibilities for peace. The other official felt the prime minister was rather idealistic and said, "The desire for peace does not necessarily insure it."

"Quite true," admitted MacDonald. "Neither does the desire for food satisfy your hunger, but at least it gets you started toward the restaurant."

Your publicity should get people to your meeting; then be sure you have something for them to "eat" after they get there.

How do you plan for a staff meeting? The respondents to the survey were equally divided when asked whether agendas for their meetings were carefully prepared and distributed in advance. Having an agenda is an essential part of effective organization and administration. The more people know about the meeting before it begins, the more effectively they can participate in the discussion. Unless you are engaging in some back-room politicking, there should be no reason why you cannot announce in advance what will be discussed.

"Also, the agenda should specify the actions which need to be taken. For example, rather than just indicating that the plans for the new educational unit will be discussed, you might want to specify that at this meeting the committee will examine and choose one of the five bids which have been received on the new building. Such an agenda entry might read something like this: 'Discussion of bids on new educational unit and selection of the most satisfactory proposal.' This way no absentee committee member can say after the meeting, 'Oh, I thought you were just going to talk about the new building some more. If I had known you were really going to make an important decision like that, I would have come.' This is all part of the strategic task of communication and *the leader must exert his best efforts to keep the members of the organization properly informed at all times" (So You Want to Be a Leader!* Kenneth O. Gangel, Christian Publications, Harrisburg, Pa.).

Memos

Though you probably don't have access to a full-time secretary, someone on your staff should serve this important facilitating role. The Sunday School superintendent, who does not see his staff sometimes for seven days at a time, especially needs to be effective in occasional written communication. One superintendent said he wrote his staff some kind of communication "45 times a year." Others responded with such statements as *not enough, not at all, monthly, infrequently, seldom,* and everything else from *once a week* to *once a year.* Perhaps the best answer is *as needed.* But then we must make careful judgments as to how frequently staff members need to hear from their superintendent.

These memos ought not always be strictly business. Get used to sending a "Thank-You-Gram" to show appreciation for the service of volunteer workers. When a response is required to a memo, you might want to indicate that you expect a reply by a certain date. Always remember that your charming smile and pleasant manner of speaking cannot come through in print, so you must depend on the words that you use and the way in which you use them to communicate graciousness and joy in your memos.

I like to combine business with public relations when handing back committee minutes. After I get the official minutes signed by the secretary and get individual copies made for all members, I take a red pen and write each committee member's name on his personalized minutes. Then I go through and check any items that he or she should be following up on during the next month. Finally, a personal note of thanks at the bottom completes the process.

Minutes

It is possible that your Sunday School staff meeting is a decision-making body. If it is, its decisions need to be duly recorded and preserved not only for posterity, but for follow-up action. These minutes ought to identify clearly what the body decided and, if possible, who was to follow up on each task.

Even if you do not make business-type decisions in a staff meeting, there is genuine merit in retaining the results of your collective discussion. The "minutes" then would be more in the form of a running commentary on what happened in the staff meeting and what conclusions, if any, came out of it.

Moments

The fourth "M" serves as an added guideline. Certainly the formal communication between the superintendent and his staff is important, but informal "moments" of conversations in the halls, office, and out on the church lawn are vital as well. As administrators, we must be constantly alert to the needs people have for our communication. On a "professional" basis, they need to have accurate and adequate information to carry out their tasks. But along with professional communication there is also personal care. In one sense the superintendent is a pastor to his staff. He does not usurp the role of the pastor, of course, but he does serve with a pastoral heart, spending himself in spiritual care of his people. Sincere inquiries about the health of a sick child or difficulties on the job will show your teachers that you care about them personally, as well as professionally (1 Thes. 2:7-12).

And don't be afraid to encourage your staff members to disagree with you. Harry Truman once said when he was president, "I want people around me who will tell me the truth as they see it." A pamphlet on administration reminds us that "letting people express their opinions doesn't reduce the boss' authority, neither does it keep him from insisting on 100% support once a final decision has been made. It simply means the boss is willing to use everybody's brains to help reach the best answer" (*Management Memo* #330, The Economics Press, Inc., Fairfield, N.J.).

Questions for Discussion

1. Review your Sunday School staff meetings for the past year. How do they measure up to the suggestions given in this chapter?

2. How about memos you have sent recently? Are they serving to motivate as well as inform those who get them?

3. Rummage through the files for minutes of recent staff meetings. Are they action-oriented? Decision-patterned? Aimed at objectives?

4. Are you satisfied with your personal times with your staff members? How can you upgrade this dimension of your ministry?

5
The Superintendent as Planner

It is impossible to say which administrative task of the Sunday School superintendent is most important. But it is certainly proper to say that planning is among the top five. Since we have dealt with the principles of the planning process elsewhere, let us concentrate here on the application of those principles to the task of the superintendent. By the way, the application of sound administrative principles in management behavior is well illustrated by Joseph's economic plan, recorded in Genesis 41.

Executive Time Investment

One principle must be reviewed: the higher the leader's place in the organization's lines of authority, the farther into the future he must project his planning. To put it another way, a Sunday School *teacher* can spend almost all of his or her time looking at this week, next week, and perhaps as far as a month or even a quarter ahead. The Sunday School *superintendent,* however, must assume that others will take the responsibility for the immediate tasks (things which he has thought about a long time ago) as he projects most of his planning from six months to a year ahead.

Perhaps the following chart can clarify the topic of planning. It is entitled "A Suggestion for Apportioning Your Thinking Time" and is adapted from an article called "Company Planning Must Be Planned," which appeared in Dun's Review and Modern Industry back in April, 1957.

Officers	Today or One Week Ahead	One Month Ahead	3-6 Mos. Ahead	One Year or More Ahead
General Superintendent	16%	20%	43%	21%
Departmental Superintendent	20%	25%	39%	16%
Teacher	78%	15%	5%	2%

But remember that good planning always looks two ways—into the past and into the future. Evaluation of what we have done before and adequate statistics regarding past performance must be compared with present needs and future projections in order to come up with intelligent plans. Planning also affects almost every area of your work: attendance, enrollment, finances, personnel, programs, equipment, facilities, and emphases. So let's look at three important steps in the planning process.

Instituting Goals

We asked the superintendents in the survey whether their Sunday Schools develop written goals annually. Only 46%, less than half, responded affirmatively to that question. This reflects back, of course, on some of the other problems indicated by the superintendents, such as worker recruitment, motivational difficulties, and stimulating individual responsibility on the part of their staff members. Too often we focus only on numerical growth, which is not the only important thing.

This is not a polemic against large churches. The point is simply this: Though a church ought to be growing in size, that growth and its representation in numbers on a bulletin board is not the *only* measure of its spiritual strength. It may not even be the *best* measure.

While on a lecture tour of South Africa, I talked with scores of pastors who had not yet captured the concept of "body life." They were judging their success almost exclusively on their churches' attendance and membership rolls. The problem is not a great deal different on the North American continent since we too have been enculturated to think of success in terms of numbers.

Churches *ought* to be evangelizing, and increased numbers ought to indicate successful evangelism. As good as that is, however, evangelism is only a portion of the total task. We tend to get trapped into a numbers game by the success-consciousness of our Western culture on the one hand and by the simple fact that numerical growth is the easiest kind to plan for and to tabulate. We can easily measure whether our Sunday School has grown from 200 to 225 in a given year. It is much more

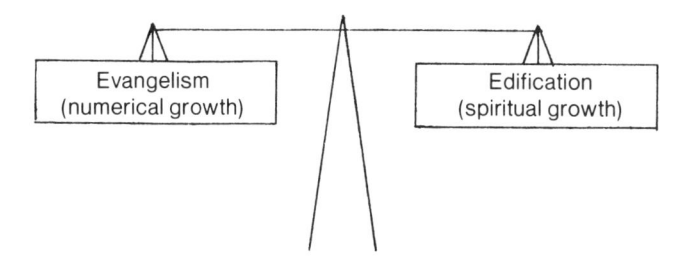

```
    ╱╲────────────╱╲            ╱╲
   ╱  ╲          ╱  ╲          ╱  ╲
  ┌─────────────┐   ╲          ┌─────────────┐
  │ Evangelism  │    ╲         │ Edification │
  │(numerical   │     ╲        │(spiritual   │
  │ growth)     │      ╲       │ growth)     │
  └─────────────┘       ╲      └─────────────┘
                         ╲
                          ╲
```

difficult to measure whether our people have experienced a comparable level of spiritual growth. Perhaps the key words are *biblical balance.*

We must plan for spiritual growth through edification of believers just as we must plan for numerical growth through the evangelization of the unsaved. Either one to the exclusion of the other is a nonbiblical emphasis. Incidentally, 90% of the superintendents surveyed indicated that their Sunday School goals were not strictly numerical and listed such things as visitation, personal growth, Bible study, and curriculum evaluation among their written goals.

Most of the churches in the United States and Canada are small. Lyle Schaller offers recent statistics: "Approximately 60% of all Protestant churches in the United States and Canada contain fewer than 200 members each, and two-thirds of them average less than 120 at worship period. In other words, at least half of all Protestant congregations on the North American continent can be classified as small" (*Preaching and Worship in the Small Church,* Willimon and Wilson, Abingdon, 1980, p. 7).

Involving People

Dr. Lois LeBar properly reminds us that "since a leader is not seeking to push through his own ideas but to guide the thinking of the group, he sees all sides of the question are fairly represented, moderates them all, then tries to help the group integrate them into common group purposes. He is flexible enough to make use of the initiative and experience of the whole group, yet firm enough to keep steering toward the goal" (*Focus on People in Church Education,* Revell, Old Tappan, N.J.). It is a basic axiom of planning that people generally assist in the implementation stage corresponding with how well they have been involved at the planning stage.

Sometimes, however, our best efforts to involve people in

their own behalf will not meet with enthusiasm. We end up feeling rather like the doctor whose telephone rang on a night when the weather was marked by heavy winds and chilling rains. The caller said that his wife needed urgent attention and requested the doctor's presence at his home immediately.

The doctor responded by saying, "I'll be glad to come, but my car is being repaired. Can you come and get me?"

In indignation the caller sputtered, "What? In this weather?"

Nevertheless, we must try to involve our people all along the way. Don't keep your teachers and workers in the dark while the staff officers of the Sunday School decide what will be done and then majestically unveil the new plan as if you were taking the wraps off a new-model car. Talk to your people—and listen to them. Include them in the planning process at the earliest possible stage. Let them tell you what their needs are in the classrooms, their difficulties with the curriculum, the reasons the visitation program doesn't seem to be clicking, and their complaints about the conduct of the monthly workers' conferences. That kind of input is just as valuable as the attendance statistics by which you will map out some of your departmental goals for the next year.

Possibly you will want to involve a special person as a "planner." Perhaps you see your other administrative tasks as being too pressing to allow you the thinking time necesary for long-range planning. Professionals in management science are increasingly using special planning experts who work hand in hand with the manager to achieve the best possible effects. Perhaps there is a man in your church who does not feel gifted or called to teach Sunday School but who has a unique sense of organization and perhaps even holds an important executive position in his company.

The key to success in such a pattern is the cooperative effort. You have the information and he has the know-how; you have the resources and he has time for this project; you have to make the choices, but he can help design the options.

Implementing Realization Procedures

How and when do we achieve strategic objectives? This is the crux of the matter. Many times we leave church business meetings feeling good about the things discussed, the ideas shared, and the decisions made. Three or four weeks later, we discover there has been no implementation. If we think about it, we probably will be able to identify the problem: We did not indicate in the meeting who was responsible to do what, and when it was to be done. The old cliché still proves true, "What is everyone's job is no one's job."

In some ways the implementation stage is the hardest on which to get general agreement. At this point we must commit ourselves to specific performance goals. We can no longer sit back in an easy chair and dream about what might be. We must now take and/or give responsibility for specific achievements. We must remember too that planning is a continuous and dynamic process. In one sense we do develop "a plan" but in another vital sense the plan is always changing, so flexibility and adaptability are important virtues in the planning process. For example, if Superintendent Joe Dunlop plans to move four Sunday School classes from rented high school facilities to the new Christian Education building by September, he may find himself in some difficulty if he has not allowed for the usual delays in construction, possible strikes, bad weather, and numerous other failures which might keep the new building from being ready until December. Or his plan for increased attendance may need revision if a major industry closes a plant in town, forcing several thousand people to move from the area.

The main thing is to specifically identify what is to be done, by whom, and when. After we have instituted the goals and involved our people in the planning process, we need to move objectively toward goal realization. Time, resources, and personnel must be blended in a single effort toward achievement (see Phil. 3:14).

Investigating Progress

Of course, we cannot tell whether we are moving objectively toward goal realization unless we build in some measurement. Evaluation is simply getting answers to the question, "How are we doing?" There are probably more clichés connected with planning than any other single administrative task, but many are still true, such as the one that reminds us to "plan your work and then work your plan."

How did the superintendents in our survey do on the matter of evaluation? About 63% depend on informal observation to determine whether goals are being reached; 20% hold an annual evaluation meeting; and 17% require written reports from their staffs. One wonders how much evaluation is actually being done by the 63%.

Questions for Discussion

1. In one paragraph write "the plan" for your Sunday School for this year. Is it workable, flexible, measurable, and people-related?

2. How effective have you been in goal-setting? Are your goals clear, brief, measurable, and specific? Do all members of your staff understand and support them?

3. Describe the balance between numerical growth and spiritual growth in your Sunday School. Are you satisfied with both?

4. Think through how a professional planning consultant might be beneficial to you and your colleagues.

6
The Superintendent as Change Agent

Bill Newland is facing a tough decision in his church. When he accepted the Sunday School superintendency two years ago on a three-year-term basis, he agreed with the Board of Christian Education that something should be done to increase the learning level in the three adult classes. Attendance had not been particularly good, slightly below average when compared with patterns in the other departments. But the lack of involvement of the people in serious Bible study was an even greater problem.

Within the first year of his superintendency, Bill announced that the traditional system of age-group divisions for adults was to be abandoned and a new department configuration would offer four electives. It was a good plan, and Bill was sincere about implementing it for the good of the Sunday School. But for the last year he has had nothing but complaining and expressions of dissatisfaction with the new elective format. He is now contemplating either switching back to the age-group divisions which the church has always used or quitting the superintendency and letting somebody else grapple with the problem.

Where did Bill go wrong?

He did not properly observe at least five crucial elements in the process of change. Since many churches have successfully switched from the traditional age-group pattern to electives in the past 10 years, there is no reason to believe that it could not have been done smoothly in Bill's Sunday School, had he been careful about his role as an administrator. Though it may seem negative and probably won't help Bill at this point, let's observe his mistakes in making the switch.

Be Patient
The change was made too soon. Bill had barely gotten into the job. His teachers and staff were just getting used to his leadership and were building up some level of confidence in what he was doing. They appreciated the fact that he was an aggressive young man, but they also knew he had no previous experience in superintending though he had been a teacher in the Junior Department for about four years.

He underestimated the level of commitment many people have to the status quo. Fear of failure, comfort in the old ways, and general misunderstanding all came back to haunt him in the early weeks after the change was adopted. There is a real possibility that he might have made the switch much more smoothly had he waited until the middle of his second year before announcing what was going to be done.

Let People Speak
The change was also too private. The decision regarding the change was unveiled as a proclamation from on high. Bill had not consulted with all the appropriate people when he thought through the issues. To be sure, he had discussed the matter with the superintendent of the Adult Department, but anyone below that level picked up the information purely from the time-honored grapevine system.

Some adults knew the change was coming and some didn't.

That alone created unrest because the story regarding the purpose for the change was distorted by those who knew and yet didn't approve. Furthermore, those adult students who didn't know were offended when they discovered that many other adults had picked up this information.

Long before a final decision was reached, Bill should have presented the plan to a combined assembly of the Adult classes, pointed out its advantages, described its objectives, asked for input, waited another several weeks while he listened for feedback, and then possibly instituted the plan on a one-year trial basis so people would not feel their bridges had been burned behind them (Col. 4:1).

Lyle Schaller refers to one of the components of cooperative ministry as "ownership" and says: "In churches with a congregational church polity it has become increasingly popular for a properly elected goal-setting committee to submit its list of suggested or recommended goals to be reviewed and adopted at a congregational meeting. This system does help establish a stronger sense of ownership among those who are on the prevailing side of every vote. However, in many cases, most of these people already had a strong sense of ownership in the suggested goals, since perhaps 12 of the difficult 23 people who bothered to come to that congregational meeting would have been members or spouses of members of the committee that formulated the recommended goals. This process does little for those—usually a majority of the membership—who stayed away and it rarely increases the sense of ownership among those on the losing side when the votes were cast" (*The Pastor and the People*, Abingdon, Nashville, Tenn.).

In Bill's case the problem was not so much a majority group and a minority group or even the matter of voting. Open communication of what the Christian Education Committee was thinking about doing and a soliciting of opinions and viewpoints regarding the change, would have been sufficient to build the sense of ownership of which Schaller speaks.

Think Small
The change was *too* big. At first glance, of course, it doesn't look very big. But size is relative to many other factors in the situation. In other words, if Bill had been working in a church which was progressive and innovative in its thinking, the switch in one department from traditional grading to an elective system might have seemed small in comparison with some of the other things going on in the church.

But his church is much more conservative and traditional in its patterns. Many of the adults have been in their age-group classes with the same clique of friends for 20 years or more. It appeared to them that Bill was challenging the validity of the way they had been doing things for many years, since the change to electives not only separated the members of classes, but teachers were reassigned, and even different classrooms were necessary because of the cyclical pattern of electives.

In Bill's church, at this time, given his short-term superintendency, the change was too big. However, had he paid careful attention to being patient and letting people speak, he could have greatly lowered the resistance level to the change. This would have made it appear smaller and less frightening to most of the people involved.

Sometimes people don't verbalize their opposition to change, but the negative attitude which results still hinders the progress of the organization. George Denny, Jr., founder and moderator of "America's Town Meeting of the Air," used to tell the story of a New York newspaper reporter who went up to Maine to interview an old fellow who was nearing his 100th birthday.

He approached the elderly gentleman politely and said, "Sir, you must have seen a great many changes during your 100 years."

The old man gazed steadily at him and replied, "Yes, and I've been against all of them."

Stay Close to Home

The change was too peripheral. You may well ask, "How could it be 'too big' and 'too peripheral' at the same time? We're not talking now about the periphery of the operation of the Sunday School, as certainly anything that affects all members in the Adult Department is a central issue. But it was too peripheral as related to Bill's area of control. Had he changed the record system or the way the superintendent presents his five-minute devotional in an opening worship session, or the format of the staff meetings, his problems would have been minimal. But in swinging into the elective system it appeared that he was meddling in an area that did not properly belong under his control.

And it made no difference that he was merely acting as the agent of the Christian Education Committee. Such a defense was no help in ameliorating the difficulties he faced. It appeared that he was simply trying to pass the buck and make excuses for himself when, after he got the flak from the adults, he indicated he was merely doing what the committee wanted him to do. After all, the change had not occurred until he became superintendent.

Hang in There!

It is axiomatic in the process of change that leaders should begin at the point of most control. And the longer one stays in a position of leadership, the more likely he is to extend his reach of control. A young pastor called to his first church, for example, probably has the authority over the subject of his sermons and a few other areas directly related to his own personal ministry. But he had better not start telling the veteran deacons that the church needs to relocate or that the

Sunday morning service will now be held 45 minutes earlier. By contrast, a veteran pastor who has ministered in the same church for 25 years may be able to influence almost every part of that congregation's life without getting into serious trouble.

Please remember that we are talking about what *is*, not necessarily what *ought to be*. You may think Bill should have complete authority to change the curriculum as he wishes. After all, what does it mean to be superintendent? But leadership, like politics, is the art of the possible. If the Sunday School superintendent is going to be a successful agent of change in his congregation, he had better observe the basic guidelines for change.

Don't Meddle

The change was too personal. As indicated above, Bill was meddling in the lives of people. It is always easier to change things than it is to change people, even though changing people is more important. Bill thought of his situation as a change of curriculum, class composition, and rooms. The people thought of it as a change of their long-time personal Sunday School habit patterns. Bill viewed the change as well within the prerogatives of the Sunday School superintendent, or at least the board of Christian education. The people demanded a sense of "ownership," being in on decisions that affected them closely.

Too often people are brought into the act *ex post facto*. That is, *after* the leader has decided what he wants done and how to go about doing it, he braces himself for what he knows will be a great difficulty in selling the plan to his constituents. The principle of commitment suggests that right at the outset an attempt be made to secure agreement to an active role in the project on the part of the members of the group. They should be saying *our* class, not *your* class, *our* church, not *your* church. In bringing about change, leadership is the process of *working with people,* not working over them, or worse yet *working them over.* (Kenneth O. Gangel, *So You Want to Be a Leader!* see p. 48)

Credibility

If you can avoid the problems that trapped Bill, you can be a positive change agent for your Sunday School. But remember that people must be informed. They must be persuaded that the change is a good one, that it is needed, and that it will work. Be a thorough communicator. Explain in detail the objectives of the new program or new idea and how the people can work together to achieve them.

Your own credibility is a most important factor. Bill acted too soon. He had not established a reputation as a credible and trusted superintendent. As a result, instead of looking like a positive innovator, he came across as a negative deviant who was trying to upset the equilibrium of what people perceived as a properly functioning Sunday School.

In "selling" a new idea, don't fail to present both sides of the case. When he appeared (or should have appeared) before the adult students in a collective assembly, Bill could have emphasized some of the values of the present system. Then he could have said that while he respected those values, the new elective system would add even more of the kinds of things people look for in a Sunday School experience.

Keep the explanation simple, break it into component parts if necessary, so people can understand it, and give them every opportunity to ask questions or make comments about what is being planned. Remember that "resistance" is usually the "persistence" of a previously successful stage of operations.

And be flexible. Its just possible that you and the fine members of your board of Christian education or the Sunday School staff have not really thought through all the implications of a change. Expect to learn from sharing your plans with others and build their requests and concerns into the final product.

Questions for Discussion

1. Think through the changes which have taken place in your Sunday School during the past year. Have they been brought about through proper processes?

2. Now look ahead. What changes need to be made during the next year? How will you avoid the pitfalls which Bill Newland fell into?

3. Discuss Schaller's view of "ownership." How does it work in your church?

4. Describe quite specifically your own "point of most control." How did you determine it? How does it affect your role as a change agent?

Conclusion

How are the Sunday Schools in our survey doing in terms of growth? Sixty-four percent of the respondents indicated that their Sunday Schools have grown in the past year, while 36% indicated they have not. The average growth percentage turned up at 16.42%. This is not typical of all Sunday Schools, but is representative of the thriving churches that responded to this survey. Though not everyone agrees that the Sunday School is healthy and growing, there seems to be some evidence that the downturn of the late '60s and '70s is behind us and Sunday Schools in the evangelical churches are rebounding in the last years of the 20th century.

A Day of Opportunity

It's a great time to be a Sunday School superintendent. The leadership role which you hold will call forth from you all that you have to put in it. Indeed, it will demand resources beyond those you have personally, so you have the joyous privilege of utilizing an unending supply of spiritual resources available from the God of the Bible.

The world is sick economically, morally, physically, emotionally, and spiritually. The "lasting peace" of which people spoke so fondly a few decades ago now seems quite shaky. Violence and terrorism are the order of the day, and the eyes of even the most secular and ungodly world leaders are focused on the Middle East and the ancient city of Jerusalem. How long will it be till the Lord returns? None of us can say, of course, but the words of Jesus Himself echo down through the halls of history: "As long as it is day, we must do the work of Him who sent Me. Night is coming, when no one can work" (John 9:4, NIV).

History seems to indicate that the light of the church shines brightest when the darkness of the world is most severe. If this is true, what a wonderful time to be called of God to lead that program of evangelism and edification which we call Sunday School. So reaffirm your call, develop your gifts, gather the troops, and let's get on with the work of the Master, in His name and in His power!

Additional Resources

Information in the following books can help make you an even better Sunday School superintendent. But Victor Books does not endorse every statement in all of these books.

Bell, A. Donald. *How to Get Along with People in the Church.* Grand Rapids, Mich.: Zondervan Publishing House, 1960.

Bower, Robert K. *Administering Christian Education.* Grand Rapids, Mich.: Wm. B. Eerdmans Publishing Co., 1964.

Gangel, Kenneth O. *Lessons in Leadership from the Bible.* Winona Lake, Ind.: BMH Books, 1980.

Gangel, Kenneth O. *Leadership for Church Education.* Chicago, Ill.: Moody Press, 1970, revised and expanded, 1981.

Gangel, Kenneth O. *So You Want to Be a Leader.* Harrisburg, Pa.: Christian Publications, 1973.

Heim, Ralph D. *Leading a Church School.* Philadelphia, Pa.: Fortress Press, 1968.

Judy, Marvin T. *The Multiple Staff Ministry.* Nashville, Tenn.: Abingdon Press, 1969.

Kilinski, Kenneth K. and Wofford, Jerry C. *Organization and Leadership in the Local Church.* Grand Rapids, Mich.: Zondervan Publishing House, 1973.

Leavitt, Guy P. *Superintend with Success.* Cincinnati, O.: Standard Publishing Company, 1960, revised, 1980.

LeBar, Lois E. *Focus on People in Church Education.* Old Tappan, N.J.: Fleming H. Revell Co., 1968.

McGavran, Donald, and Hunter, George C. *Church Growth Strategies that Work.* Nashville: Abingdon, 1980.

Richards, Lawrence O. (ed.). *The Key to Sunday School Achievement.* Chicago, Ill.: Moody Press, 1965.

Schaller, Lyle E. *The Decision-Makers.* Nashville, Tenn.: Abingdon Press, 1974.

Schaller, Lyle E. *The Multiple Staff and the Larger Church.* Nashville: Abingdon, 1980.

Walrath, Douglas A. *Leading Churches through Change.* Nashville: Abingdon, 1979.

Wedel, Leonard E. *Building and Maintaining a Church Staff.* Nashville, Tenn.: Broadman Press, 1966.

Westing, Harold J. *The Super Superintendent.* Denver: Accent Books, 1980.

Westing, Harold J. *Make Your Sunday School Grow through Evaluation.* Wheaton, Ill.: Victor Books, 1976.

Wolff, Richard. *Man at the Top.* Wheaton, Ill.: Tyndale House, Publishers, 1969.